IT WORKS!
Revolution in
Computers

Cari Jackson

mc **Marshall Cavendish**
Benchmark
New York

This edition first published in 2010 in the United States
of America by Marshall Cavendish Benchmark.

Marshall Cavendish Benchmark
99 White Plains Road
Tarrytown, NY 10591
www.marshallcavendish.us

All Internet addresses were available and accurate when this book went to press.

Library of Congress Cataloging-in-Publication Data

Jackson, Cari.
Revolution in computers / by Cari Jackson.
p. cm. -- (It works!)
Summary: "Discusses the history of computers, how the technology
was developed, and the science behind it"--Provided by publisher.
Includes bibliographical references and index.
ISBN 978-0-7614-4375-9
1. Computers-- History--Juvenile literature. I. Title.
QA76.23 I26 2010
004--dc22
2008054517

Cover: Q2AMedia Art Bank
Half Title: Shutterstock.
P7: Photocreo Michal Bednarek/Shutterstock; P11: Lisa F. Young/Shutterstock;
P15cr: Kayella/Dreamstime; P15br: Ethan Myerson/iStockphoto;
P19: Dreamstime; P23: Lisa Young/123RF; P27: Shutterstock.
Illustrations: Q2AMedia Art Bank

Created by Q2AMedia
Series Editor: Jessica Cohn
Art Director: Sumit Charles
Client Service Manager: Santosh Vasudevan
Project Manager: Shekhar Kapur
Designer: Shilpi Sarkar
Illustrators: Aadil Ahmed, Rishi Bhardwaj,
Kusum Kala, Parwinder Singh and Sanyogita Lal
Photo research: Sakshi Saluja

Printed in Malaysia

135642

Contents

Monster Computer

How fast is the population growing? How long is Earth's path around the Sun? Before computers, people had to work together to solve difficult problems like these. It took a long time to figure out the numbers.

Howard Aiken did research in the 1930s. He needed a **calculator** that could do many math problems quickly. Aiken was stuck. Then he heard about Charles Babbage. Babbage had lived one hundred years earlier. Babbage had made plans for that kind of machine. Aiken used Babbage's research. He added his own ideas. In May 1944, Aiken presented the Harvard Mark I. It was 8 feet high (2.5 meters) and 2 feet (.60 meters) deep. It weighed 5 tons (4 tonnes). The world's most famous computer had been born.

Meet Howard Aiken

Howard Aiken was not afraid of extra work. He was born in 1900 in Hoboken, New Jersey. In high school, he worked twelve hours every night after school. He then studied at Harvard University. That's where he came up with his idea for the Harvard Mark I. In nineteen hours, the Mark I could complete a math problem that took four people three weeks to do. Konrad Zuse was a German inventor. He had invented a faster computer several years earlier. Few people knew about it, though. So Mark I became the most famous "first" modern computer. The computer revolution happened fast after that! Within two years, newer computers were hundreds of times faster.

A paper tape with instructions runs through the machine. I can change the instructions as needed.

I tell the calculator what numbers to use by putting in paper that's punched a certain way.

The Mark I can work with numbers with twenty-three places. It can add or subtract two of those numbers in three-tenths of a second.

It can multiply them in four seconds and divide them in ten seconds.

Debate!

pencil and paper

partner or small group

1 Computers perform many services. Some of these services, such as music sharing, have raised problems, however. There are legal and illegal ways to share music, after all. Some people say sharing music with other people should be legal no matter what. Other people say sharing music is stealing. You be the judge.

2 **Yes:** If a kid shares a toy, the kid's friend doesn't have to pay the toy company. If I buy a CD, I should be able to share it. Other people should be able to share their music with me. That way, more people hear the music. More people want to go to the band's concerts. That helps bands become more popular. Sharing music on the **Internet** does the same thing.

3 **No:** Songs, books, and drawings each have a **copyright**. All published material has a copyright. Only the person who owns the copyright has the right to make copies of the material. That person can decide if it is for sale or public use. That's how artists, musicians, and writers make money. If you make a copy of a song and give it away, that's stealing.

4 Music companies have sued kids as young as twelve for sharing music illegally. What do you think? Discuss both sides. Have one person take one side. Have another person take the other. Write the reasons for both sides on a piece of paper.

WHO WOULD HAVE THOUGHT?

Music Sharing

The military and government had the best computers first. When people outside the military got their own computers, they quickly linked with others all over the world. One of the first things people did was to store and swap music.

Shawn Fanning was a college freshman in 1999. He created a free music service called Napster. Fanning's service did not store millions of songs in one place. Instead, Fanning wrote a special computer program. The program allowed people to **download** music from other computers. The music was shared over the Internet. Most music is copyrighted, however. It is illegal to swap it for free. Music companies and musicians sued Napster and won. Now you have to pay to use Napster. New kinds of communication always raise new questions!

Music is just a click away.

Winning Program

Only a few people could even touch the big, early computers. An even smaller number knew how to write programs. These are instructions that computers understand. Computers read programs in **binary code**. That code looks like a weird series of numbers. Different signs, letters, or numbers stand for other signs, numbers, or commands.

Grace Murray Hopper wrote some of the first programs for the Mark I. This kind of work became known as computer programming. Soon it was clear that the world would keep finding more uses for computers. Hopper, with help, came up with a programming language more people could use. The new language was called **COBOL**. That is short for Common Business-Oriented Language. COBOL was written in English. Now, millions of people would be able to understand "computer talk."

Meet Grace Murray Hopper

Grace Murray Hopper was born in New York City in 1906. She loved to play with gadgets. She once took apart seven alarm clocks. Hopper later became a math professor. Then she joined the Navy. There, she began writing programs for the Mark I. Hopper was outstanding in the computer science field.

Hopper came up with the term *computer bug*. One day, the Mark I was acting up. Hopper checked the switches. She finally found the problem: a poor, beaten-to-death moth. From then on, whenever the computer acted up, Hopper would say she was "debugging" it.

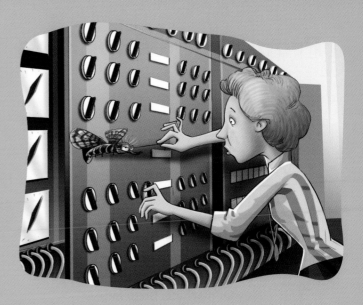

A computer understands commands written in binary code. That's a language written in 0's and 1's. For instance, "00110101" might mean "Add." When the computer reads "00110101," it adds the numbers.

My job is to turn a difficult math problem into simple steps. I may have to write 50 steps in 0's and 1's just to tell the computer to do one math problem.

The COBOL program turns binary code into English. Say a business needs to take taxes out of someone's paycheck. The COBOL programmer can write, "SUBTRACT TAXES FROM PAY."

A program in the computer understands COBOL. It changes the command into binary code. The computer says, "Ah, I understand!" This happens in an instant.

Programming for Kids

computer

adult helper

Note: This activity was written for Netlogo 4.0.3. It's possible that this program won't work on later versions of Netlogo. If that happens, ask an adult to help you download the new Netlogo. Then try to do an activity like this one.

 1 Ask an adult to help you get Netlogo on your machine. Go to http://ccl.northwestern.edu/netlogo/download.shtml. Download Netlogo, install it, and then run it.

 2 Click on the Procedures tab after it is running. Then type in the following commands exactly as you see them here.

To draw a red square:

create-turtles 1
ask turtles [
set heading 0
set color red
pen-down
forward 10
right 90
forward 10
right 90
forward 10
right 90
forward 10

 3 Switch to the Interface tab. At the bottom of the window, find it shows: "observer>" . . . . Type: Draw-a-red-square

 4 Press the Enter key. You just used a programming language to command your computer to draw a red square. Once you understand how to use the Netlogo language, you can make your computer do all sorts of things!

WHO WOULD HAVE THOUGHT?

Personal Computers

In the 1960s, personal computers (PCs) didn't even exist. Mathematicians wrote programs. Regular people did not. The idea that a programming language could be simple enough for kids seemed crazy.

Seymour Papert knew that computers could be learning tools for kids. Papert came up with Logo. Logo is a programming language. It can do many things, yet it is easy to understand. Kids could type in Logo commands. They could tell a "turtle" on the screen how to draw shapes. That helped kids understand the concept of programming. Today, the language is called Netlogo. This special language can command a turtle on the screen to do things. You can practice and get good at it. You can use Netlogo for big projects, such as making music or art.

Computers are good for schoolwork.

Smaller Is Faster

Scientists wanted to make computers smaller. How would that be done? Computers needed more than a million parts! Jack Kilby and Robert Noyce, working separately, came up with a solution. They invented the **integrated circuit**, or **chip**, in the 1950s. That made computers faster. How? Chips cut the distance electricity has to travel inside the machines.

Electricity travels at the speed of light. There's no way it can go any faster. **Electrical circuits** send information using electricity. The circuits have many parts that have to be connected. Kilby and Noyce both realized that making all the parts out of the same material would be helpful. Then the materials could be put on one block. That block could be tiny. The electricity would not have far to go. Computers could become lightning fast. They were right!

Meet Jack Kilby and Robert Noyce

Jack Kilby and Robert Noyce were born in the Midwest. Kilby was born in 1923. Noyce was born in 1927. Kilby was shy. They both studied **physics** at separate colleges. Noyce ran Fairchild Semiconductor. Kilby worked for Texas Instruments.

Kilby invented the chip in the summer of 1958. That was just a few months before Noyce came up with the same idea. Noyce ended up solving problems in Kilby's invention. For instance, Noyce thought of painting on metal strips instead of using wires. Computers that once were the size of a room could suddenly fit on a playing card. The chip made it possible to travel to the moon!

A circuit has a part that acts like a switch. It can turn electrical current on or off. It can make current stronger. The circuit also has parts that store information.

All of a circuit's parts have to be made separately. The parts have to be connected with wire. If the wires break, the current will stop.

Silicon is an element found on Earth. It may be the answer. This material doesn't conduct electricity well on its own. If we add other elements to it, though, it can!

We can build all the parts on one silicon block. Different parts of the silicon can serve different purposes. We can paint on strips of metal, and good-bye, wires!

Salt Wired

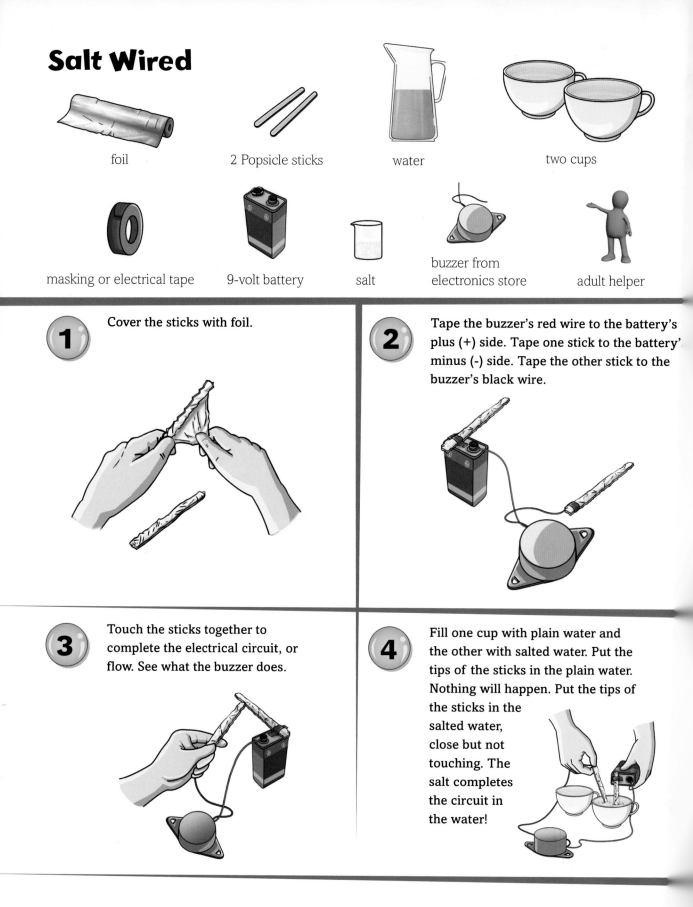

foil

2 Popsicle sticks

water

two cups

masking or electrical tape

9-volt battery

salt

buzzer from electronics store

adult helper

1 Cover the sticks with foil.

2 Tape the buzzer's red wire to the battery's plus (+) side. Tape one stick to the battery' minus (-) side. Tape the other stick to the buzzer's black wire.

3 Touch the sticks together to complete the electrical circuit, or flow. See what the buzzer does.

4 Fill one cup with plain water and the other with salted water. Put the tips of the sticks in the plain water. Nothing will happen. Put the tips of the sticks in the salted water, close but not touching. The salt completes the circuit in the water!

WHO WOULD HAVE THOUGHT?

One Chip in Charge

Chips made computers smaller, but not small enough. Each chip was programmed to perform separate jobs. That meant computers needed many chips. In 1971, Marcian "Ted" Hoff fixed that. Hoff was working for Robert Noyce at Intel. Hoff came up with an idea for a chip that could be programmed. He called that kind of chip a **microprocessor**. Before microprocessors, you needed a different chip for every use. Now, a single chip can perform many jobs. A computer needs only one of these microprocessors.

Now, microprocessors are everywhere. They are in cars, cell phones, and cameras. They are in calculators and pacemakers. They are even in vending machines!

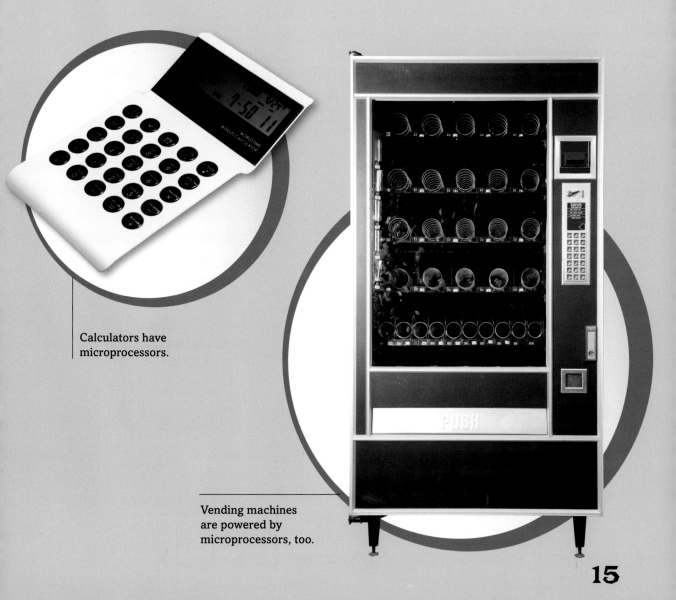

Calculators have microprocessors.

Vending machines are powered by microprocessors, too.

Computers Get Personal

In 1975, the first personal computer was sold. That computer was called the Altair 8800. It came as a kit. Only people who used computers as a hobby thought to buy it. Once you put it together, you couldn't do much with it.

Bill Gates was in college then. He knew that if he wrote the right program for the Altair 8800, more people would use it. He and his friend Paul Allen started the company Microsoft. The company made **software**. Software programs tell a computer what to do.

Meanwhile, Steve Jobs was thinking along the same lines. He wanted to sell personal computers as a unit, not a kit. That way, more people would buy them. He and his friend Steve Wozniak started the Apple computer company. The personal computer revolution had begun!

Meet Bill Gates and Steve Jobs

Bill Gates and Steve Jobs were both born in 1955. Both grew up on the West Coast. Both got interested in computers during middle school.

Gates created the Windows OS. He sold his OS to other computer companies. Jobs's company made its own OS for its computers. They were called MACs.

The competition between the companies became known as the PC vs MAC wars. (Computers that use Windows are called PCs, for "personal computers.")

A computer can't do anything without software. The main software allows a user to tell a computer what to do. Then it tells the central unit how to display the information on the screen.

The main software is the **operating system (OS)**. The OS also allows other software to run on the computer. Software that helps you write your homework, for example, runs on the OS.

Many people thought the software should be free. However, we needed to be paid for our work. We needed to pay our employees.

Do You Speak Computer?

A 01000001	H 01001000	O 01001111	V 01010110
B 01000010	I 01001001	P 01010000	W 01010111
C 01000011	J 01001010	Q 01010001	X 01011000
D 01000100	K 01001011	R 01010010	Y 01011001
E 01000101	L 01001100	S 01010011	Z 01011010
F 01000110	M 01001101	T 01010100	
G 01000111	N 01001110	U 01010101	

paper and pencil   partner   chart, provided here

1 First, come up with a short message, such as, I SPEAK COMPUTER. Do not tell your partner what the message is.

2 Rewrite your message, using the binary code chart shown here. Don't make any mistakes, or else your partner won't be able to decode it!

3 Ask your partner to decode the message.

4 Check with your partner. Did you both get it right? If not, can you find the mistakes?

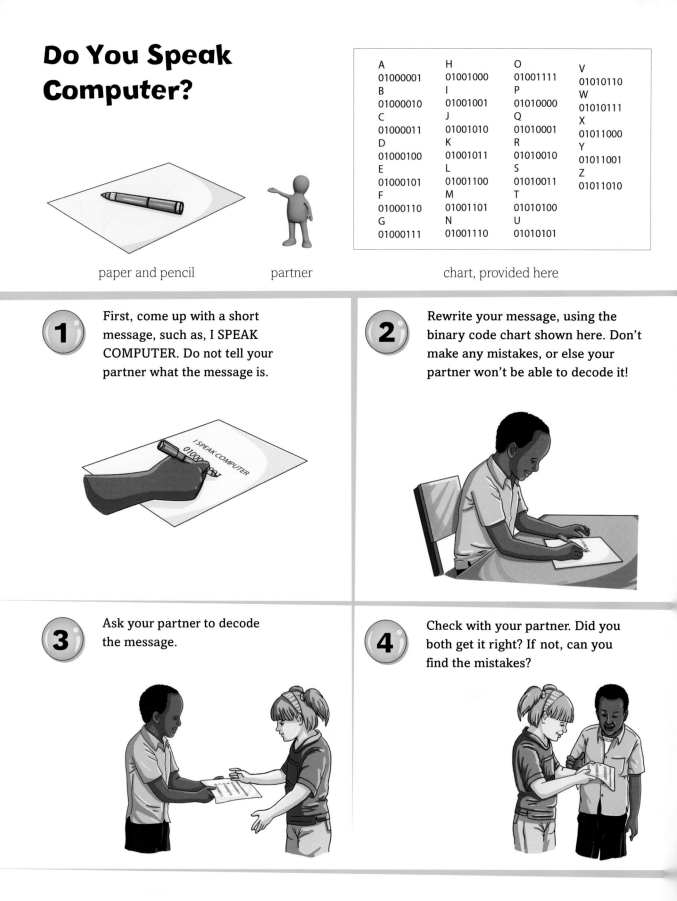

WHO WOULD HAVE THOUGHT?

Computers Keep Changing

In the late '80s, Apple started losing money. New leaders in the company blamed Steve Jobs, the founder. They pushed him out of Apple. Later, they found they needed his talent for making their products exciting. They put him in charge again. For every new computer invention, Jobs figured out a way to make Apple's version seem cooler. Suddenly, Apple could compete with the other companies again.

The iMac computer looks like a colorful bubble. The iBook laptop has a sleek design. The iPod looks like a toy from the future. It allows you to carry nearly all of your music with you. What could possibly come next? The people who will make those changes are in school now. Maybe one day you will make an even better computer product than Bill Gates or Steve Jobs ever did.

You can read books on computers.

Getting Connected

Throughout history, people wondered: What if all knowledge could be stored in one place? What if anyone could get to this knowledge and use it?

In the 1960s, a government group invented the Internet. The Internet connects computers worldwide through phone and cable lines. If one line breaks, the information finds another route. It never stops working. People started posting thousands of files on the Internet. It became a big mess. Then Tim Berners-Lee found a way to organize the information. He called it the **World Wide Web**. On August 6, 1991, he posted the first **website**. It told people what the Web was and how to use it. It was a dream come true. People could go to one place for knowledge. Today, people can read and shop online. They can even visit friends and family online. What would we do without it?

Meet Tim Berners-Lee

Tim Berners-Lee was born in London in 1955. His parents were both mathematicians. They taught him math everywhere, even at the dinner table! Numerous people came up with ways to search the Internet. However, most people thought of each item as you would a book in a library. They thought of each item as separate. They made people pay for their services. Berners-Lee did two things. First, he invented links. That was a huge step. It was as if people could put their finger on a word in a book and another book would appear with new information! He made these links happen online. Berners-Lee also made his ideas free. His way of using the Internet lasted. Many other ideas about using the Internet died out.

Every computer hooked up to the Internet has a **protocol**. This program tells computers how to communicate with each other. Each computer has an address, so that every computer can be found.

We have programs that allow users to find content on the World Wide Web. We have places that can store the websites.

A user types a web address in the right place. That sends a message. It asks for a connection.

We can link text to other text. You click on a link and get connected. The links create a "web" of information.

Right Way to Surf

The Internet is an amazing tool. You should know, however, how to protect your personal information online. You need to be aware of other people's feelings, too. This short quiz helps you think about the right way to surf. Note your answers on a piece of paper. The correct answers are upside down below the final box.

paper and pencil

---

1 What information is OK to post on a personal page?

a. Your full name and address
b. Your Social Security number
c. None of the above

---

2 If someone says something creepy online, what should you do?

a. Tell an adult. Report the behavior to the website.
b. Write back. Keep the conversation going.
c. Take your personal page down. Hope they leave you alone.

---

3 If you decide to delete something on your personal page, can anyone view it again?

a. No, it disappears forever.
b. Yes, anyone who saw the older version can still see it on that computer.

---

4 What if you have an embarrassing photo of someone?

a. If it is funny, I'll post it on my page.
b. I will e-mail it to just one other person.
c. I will delete it.

Answers: 1. c; 2. a; 3. b; 4. c

WHO WOULD HAVE THOUGHT?

Social Networks

In 1997 the first social networking site showed up. It was called SixDegrees.com. People could post information about themselves. They could find online friends who shared their interests. The popularity of these sites took off. Soon other sites popped up. They include Friendster, MySpace, Facebook, Twitter, and others. MySpace alone has more than 100 million members.

Social networking sites have their downside. Strangers approach kids online. People post too much information about themselves. Sometimes criminals steal that information. They can use it to buy things in other people's names. Kids post gossip and bully other kids. Bottom line: It is smart to be smart while online. It pays to be nice, as well. Experts say, don't post anything you wouldn't want a stranger, or your mom, to know.

Let an adult know if you go online.

Be Real

Jaron Lanier is the father of **virtual reality**. He created virtual worlds. They seem real but are not. Through computer programs, he created landscapes people could see, touch, hear, and walk through. The landscapes are fake but seem very real.

Lanier built a special helmet and gloves. The helmet puts images in front of a user's eyes. The helmet makes sounds for the user's ears. The gloves put pressure on the person's hands, as if he or she were touching real objects. Lanier often warns that fantasy is no substitute for real life. Yet virtual reality can be fun, and useful, too.

Surgeons use virtual reality to learn how to operate on people. Pilots use it to learn how to fly planes. Lanier also invented the first **avatar**. An avatar is the person on-screen in a virtual world who stands for and is controlled by the computer user.

Meet Jaron Lanier

Jaron Lanier was born in 1960, in New York City. He grew up in New Mexico. He has been called one of the greatest inventors of all time. Don't call him just an inventor, however. He is also a writer and musician. He plays piano and many other instruments. He has performed throughout the world. Lanier even uses his virtual reality machines to play music! He programs his machines so that they make the sounds of different instruments. Then, Lanier practices, using his machines. He works on the music until it is good, just as someone would with a real trumpet or guitar.

Each eye sees a slightly different view of whatever you are looking at.

Your eyes actually see two separate images. Your brain puts the two images together.

When your brain puts the images together, the image becomes **three-dimensional**.

The three dimensions are height, width, and depth. I can create images like that using software and special equipment.

3-D Eyeglasses

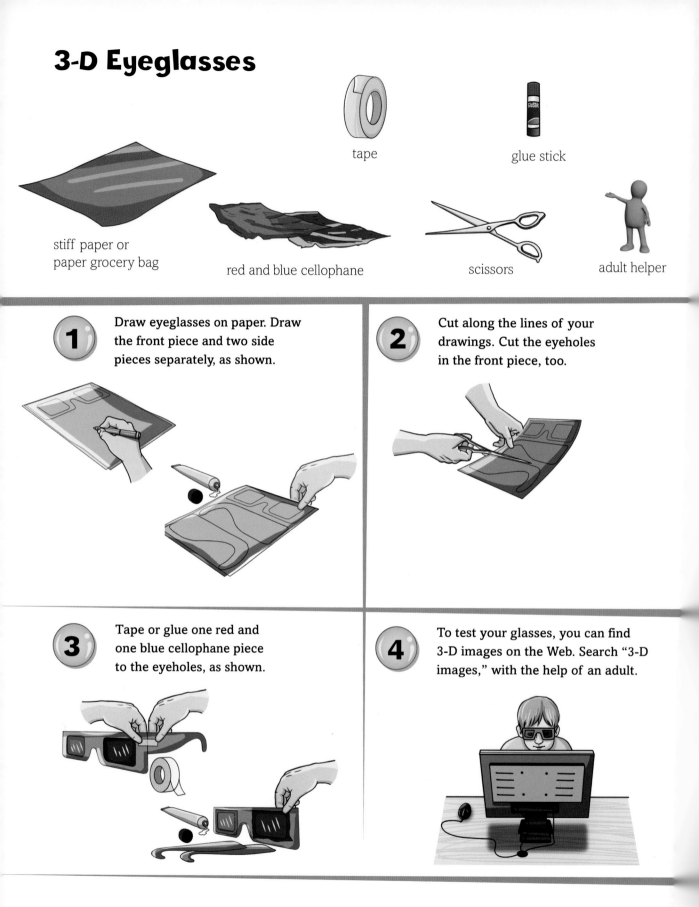

tape

glue stick

stiff paper or
paper grocery bag

red and blue cellophane

scissors

adult helper

1 Draw eyeglasses on paper. Draw the front piece and two side pieces separately, as shown.

2 Cut along the lines of your drawings. Cut the eyeholes in the front piece, too.

3 Tape or glue one red and one blue cellophane piece to the eyeholes, as shown.

4 To test your glasses, you can find 3-D images on the Web. Search "3-D images," with the help of an adult.

WHO WOULD HAVE THOUGHT?

Games to Go

The Internet is filled with games you can download. You just need to get your parents' permission. Video games have come a long way in a short time. In 1972, Atari came out with *PONG*. *PONG* was table tennis on a TV screen. People went crazy for it. The early gaming systems had only one game. Later, game cartridges were made with chips in them. Kids could plug in different cartridges to play new games. Today's gaming systems use CDs. Some of the systems hook up to the Internet. That allows gamers around the world to play one another. Millions of people play games on the Internet. Some of these games are like acting out a story online. We've come a long way since the Harvard Mark I.

Many games are made for computers.

Timeline

1944
Howard Aiken presents the Harvard Mark I.

1958–1959
Robert Noyce and Jack Kilby invent the integrated circuit, or chip.

1959
Grace Hopper and her coworkers write the COBOL programming language.

1968
Seymour Papert and his team develop LOGO programming language.

1969
Researches at ARPA, a government agency, invent the Internet.

1971
The first e-mail is sent.

1971
Marcian "Ted" Hoff invents the microprocessor.

1972
Atari starts selling *PONG*, the first successful video game.

2007
First iPhone sold.

2001
First iPod sold.

1999
Shawn Fanning creates Napster.

1997
First social networking site, SixDegrees.com, starts.

1991
Tim Berners-Lee posts the first website and creates the World Wide Web.

1980
Jaron Lanier comes up with the term *virtual reality*.

1976
Steve Jobs and Steve Wozniak found Apple.

1975
The first Altair 8800 is sold.

1975
Bill Gates and Paul Allen found Microsoft.

Glossary

avatar a digital stand-in or representation for someone real.

binary code computer code that expresses numbers, letters, and symbols using only the digits 0 and 1.

calculator an electronic machine that processes numbers.

copyright the exclusive right to publish or sell a work, such as a book.

chip an integrated circuit; an electronic device that performs many functions on a single wafer.

COBOL Common Business-Oriented Language; the most widely used programming language today.

download to transfer a file from one computer device or the Internet to another computer.

electrical circuit closed path through which an electric current travels.

integrated circuit a chip; an electronic device that performs many functions on a single wafer.

Internet worldwide collection of computers and networks that use protocols to communicate with one another through phone and cable lines.

microprocessor a chip that contains the central processing unit.

operating system (OS) the most basic program in a computer; all computers have an OS to turn the machine on and off and run other software programs.

physics science of matter and energy.

protocol a program that sets the rules two computers must follow to exchange messages.

silicon element used to make chips; it can be found in sand or quartz.

software programs that tell the computer how to do certain tasks, such as word processing; software has to be written for a specific computer OS.

three-dimensional having height, width, and depth.

virtual reality software-created environment that allows a user to sense his or her surroundings while making actions within the surroundings.

website collection of electronic pages that can contain text, images, and videos.

World Wide Web often referred to as WWW or the Web; a system of linked information on the Internet that can be accessed with software called a "browser."

To Learn More

Books

A Kid's Guide to Creating Web Pages for Home and School by Benjamin Selfridge and Peter Selfridge. Zephyr Press, 2004.

Robot (DK Eyewitness Books) by Roger Bridgman. DK Children, 2004.

Steve Jobs, Steve Wozniak, and the Personal Computer by Donald B. Lemke. Capstone Press, 2006.

Websites

Tim Berners-Lee answers kids' questions about the World Wide Web.
www.w3.org/People/Berners–Lee/Kids

Computer History Museum helps you explore the history of computers.
http://www.computerhistory.org/

Kaboose offers online lessons about computers, along with related worksheets.
http://parenting.kaboose.com/education-and-learning/learningresources/brain-computer-lesson.html

Lissa Explains It All helps kids of all ages build their own websites.
http://www.lissaexplains.com/

Index